# BLOCK CODING

BY JILL SHERMAN

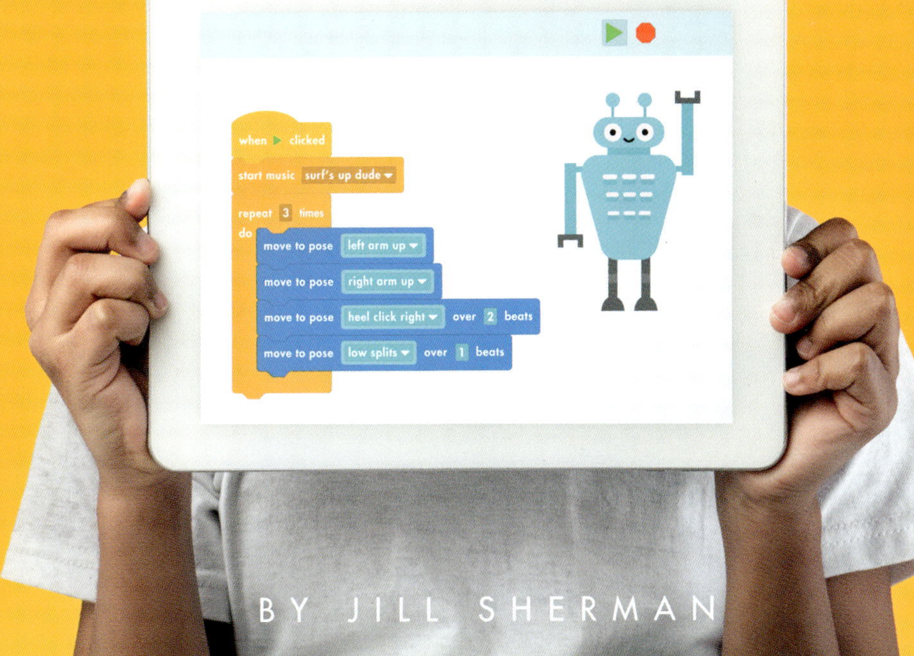




AMICUS LEARNING

# What are you

# curious about?

Curious About is published by
Amicus Learning, an imprint of Amicus
P.O. Box 227, Mankato, MN 56002
www.amicuspublishing.us



Editor: Ana Brauer
Series Designer: Kathleen Petelinsek
Book Designer and Photo Researcher: Emily Dietz

Library of Congress Cataloging-in-Publication Data
Names: Sherman, Jill, author.
Title: Curious about block coding / by Jill Sherman.
Description: Mankato, MN : Amicus Learning, [2026] | Series:
Curious about coding | Includes bibliographical references and
index. | Audience term: Children | Audience term: School children
| Audience: Ages 6–9 | Audience: Grades 2–3 | Summary:
"What is block coding? Learn about coding and programming
with block codes in this question-and-answer book for elementary
readers. Includes table of contents, glossary, books and websites
for further research, and index"— Provided by publisher.
Identifiers: LCCN 2024048326 (print) | LCCN 2024048327
(ebook) | ISBN 9798892004954 (library binding) | ISBN
9798892005494 (paperback) | ISBN 9798892006033 (ebook)
Subjects: LCSH: Computer programming—Juvenile literature.
Classification: LCC QA76.6115 .S528 2026  (print) | LCC
QA76.6115  (ebook) | DDC 005.13—dc23/eng/20250117
LC record available at https://lccn.loc.gov/2024048326
LC ebook record available at https://lccn.loc.gov/2024048327

Photo Credits: Freepik/freepik, 3, 21; Getty Images/FatCamera,
13, urbazon, 6; Scratch/unknown, 11, 14; Shutterstock/
ajt, 17, AlesiaKan, 2, 11, 19, antoniodiaz, 9, Chay_Tee,
2, 5, Designsells, cover, 1, 4, Dragon Images, 16, Heena
Rajput, 12, New Africa, 14–15, Ortis, 8, Pixel-Shot, 18,
Prostock-studio, cover, 1; The Noun Project/Y, 22, 23

# What is block coding?

Computer code is normally written as text. Block code is used to make coding simple. It is a coding language that uses drag-and-drop blocks. Each block is a piece of code. Stack the blocks to create a **program**!

## CONTROL THAT ROBOT!

Read this piece of block code. What do you think the robot will do if you click the play button?

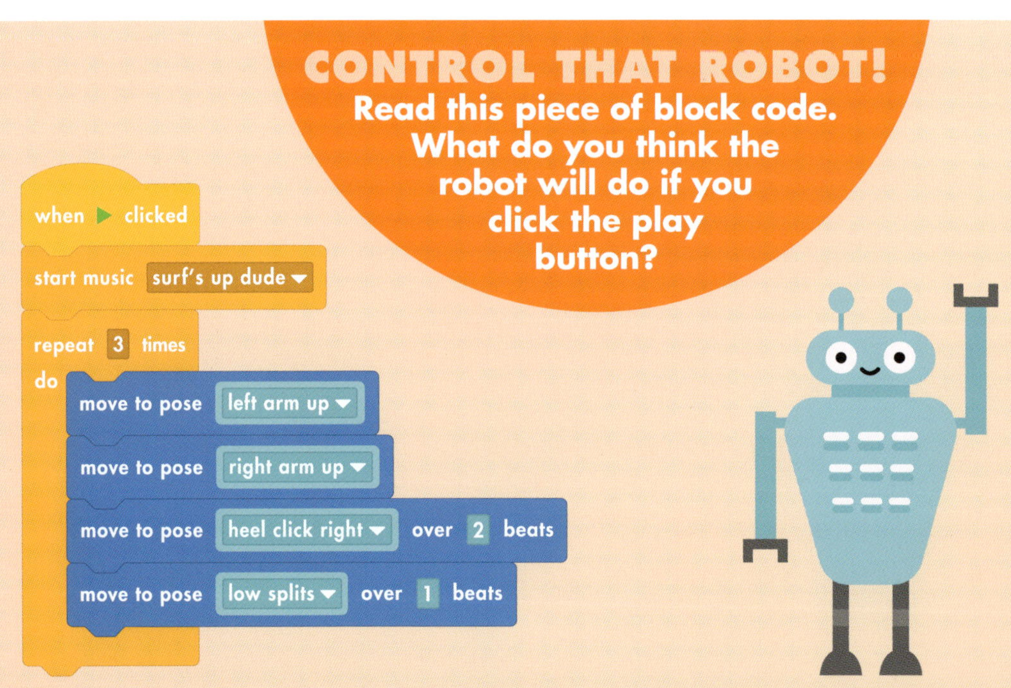

Block coding makes learning how to code easy.

Anyone can learn how to code and program a computer.

# What does code do?

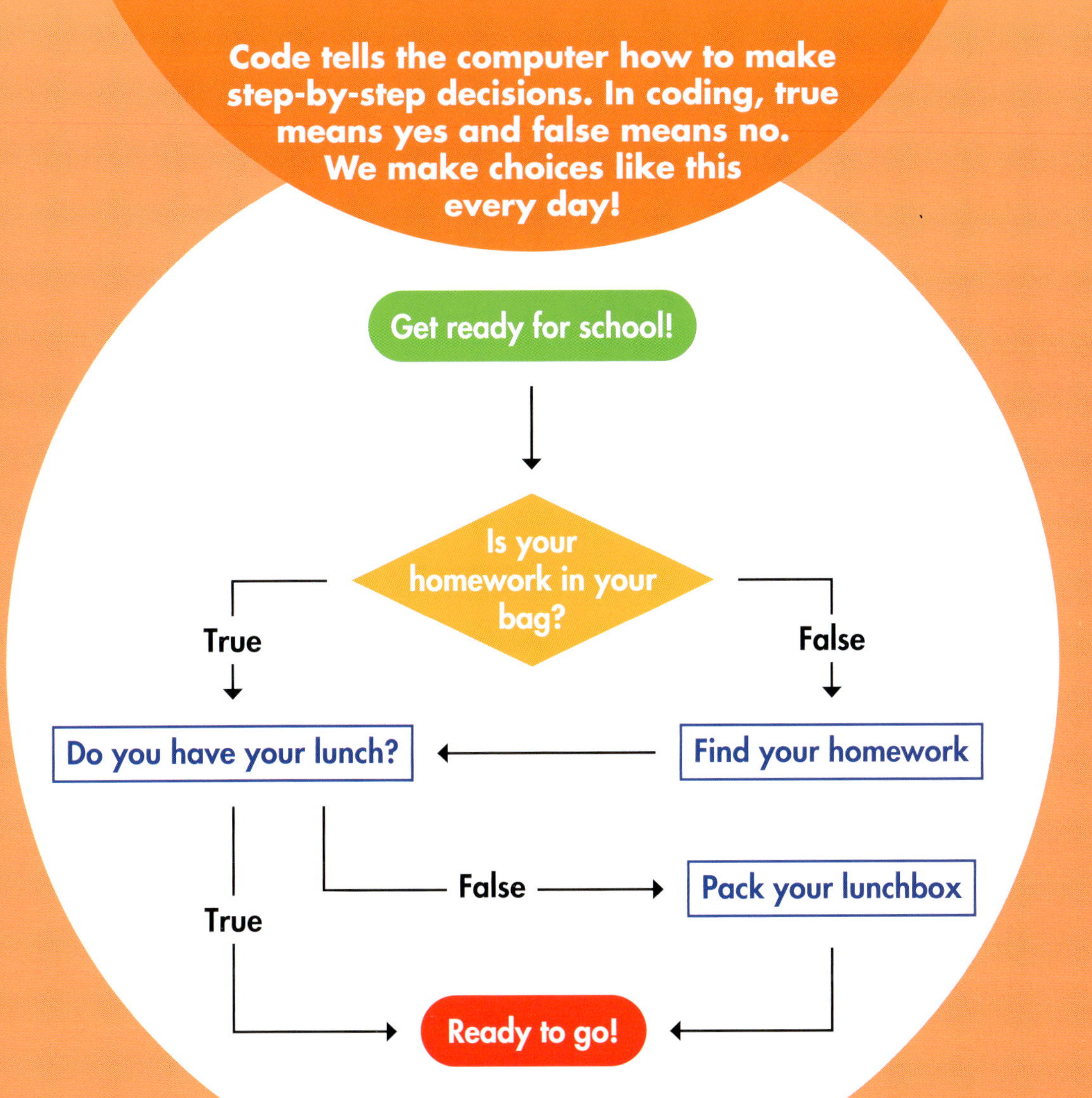




Code is the language we use to talk to a computer. It tells the computer what to do! Computers are machines. They need instructions to work. Without code, a computer couldn't do anything! You click your mouse on an icon. What happens next? It's all written in the code.

# Don't you have to be good at math to code?

No! A computer is like a very fast calculator. It does math really quickly! Writing code is more like solving a puzzle. You just need to be good at logic. You figure out the steps to make a program run.

## CODE IS EVERYWHERE

Many modern devices need coding to work. Smartphones, microwaves, and traffic lights all use code!

It's up to you
to put the pieces
of a code together.

# How do I get started with block coding?

Many **platforms** use block codes! Scratch, Code.org, and Blockly are common examples. Go to a website and pick a **tutorial** that looks fun! Start dragging and snapping blocks together. Then press run and watch what happens. Don't worry about mistakes. You can always fix them and try again!

Scratch is often used in classrooms.

## POPULAR SCRATCH CHARACTERS

# Why did my code do THAT?

**Bugs** stop your code from working properly.

Coding mistakes are called bugs. They cause the code to do something you didn't expect. Maybe the wrong thing shows on the screen. Or maybe it doesn't work at all! As a coder, it's your job to find and fix these mistakes.

Mistakes are common in coding. Keep running tests until you can fix the bug.

LET'S BUILD SOMETHING!

# What can I build with block code?

A lot of cool things! You can design fun games that you can play with your friends. You can make awesome **animations** that move and change colors. You can even program simple robots to do cool tricks!

You can make and play different games using block codes.

CHAPTER THREE

# I'm stuck! How do I get help with my code?

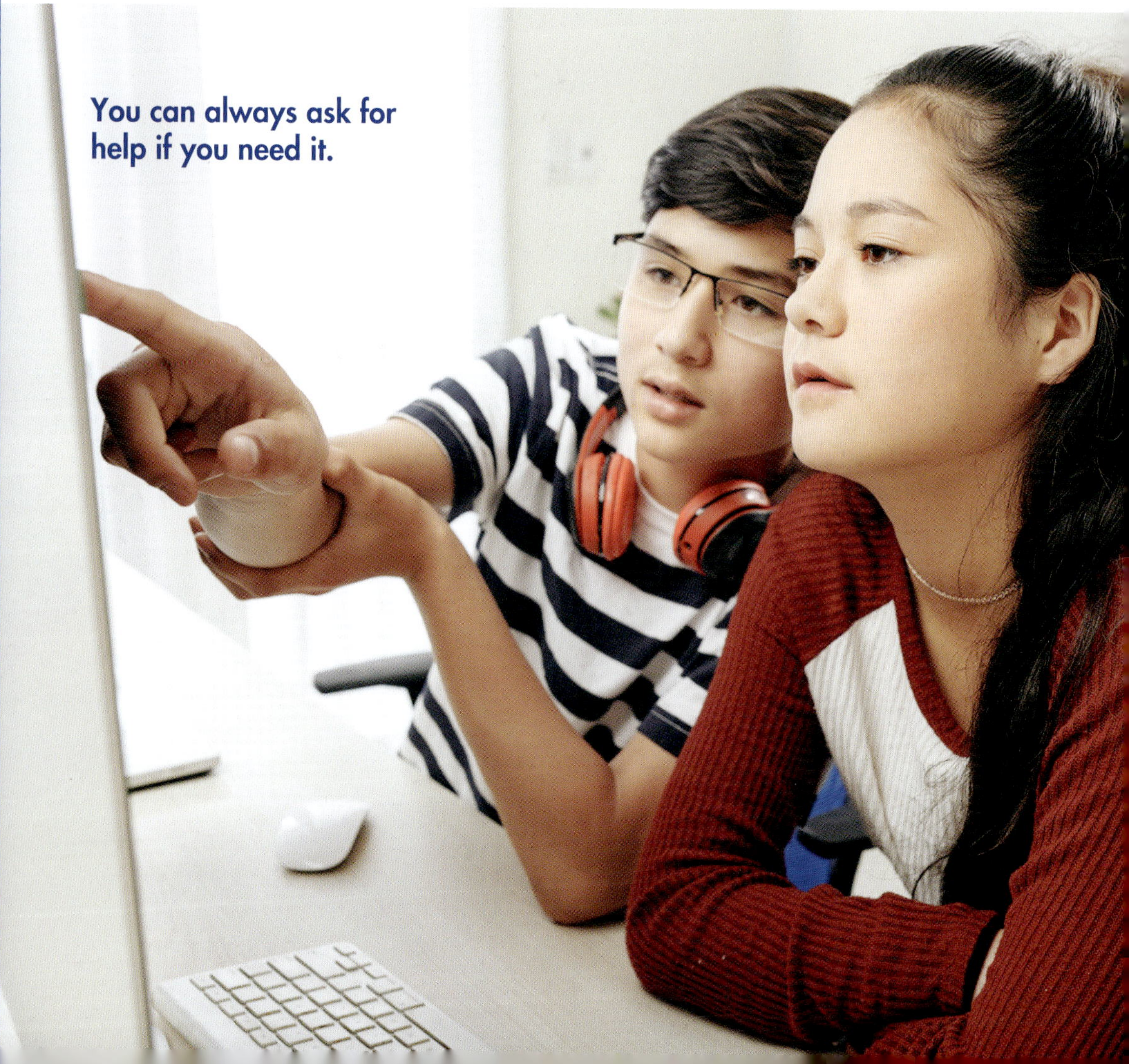

You can always ask for help if you need it.

Every coder gets stuck. It happens a LOT! Coding may look like something you do alone. But many people work together to solve problems. That's why it's fun to learn coding with friends. You can help each other!

# Is it okay to use someone else's code?

Yes! Many coders share their code for free. You can learn from their work. Study their code. You can also copy their code and **remix** it. Use their code to make something of your own!

Block codes can be used
to program a drone.

# How can I show my code projects to my friends?

First, make sure that your code is saved. You could save the project on your computer. Or you can use a special link to share it online. Ask your friends to test the code. Then think about what you want to build next.

You and your friends can test each other's codes.
CODING COMMUNITY

## ASK MORE QUESTIONS

**What are some other coding languages?**

**What jobs can coding help me get when I grow up?**

**Try a BIG QUESTION: What things are easier for humans to do than computers?**

## SEARCH FOR ANSWERS

**Search the library catalog or the Internet.**
A librarian, teacher, or parent can help you.

**Using Keywords**
Find the looking glass.

**Keywords are the most important words in your question.**

?

**If you want to know about:**

- different coding languages, type: CODING LANGUAGES

- what jobs use coding, type: CODING JOBS

# FIND GOOD SOURCES

## Here are some good, safe sources you can use in your research.
Your librarian can help you find more.

### Books

**Coding and Programming**
by Nancy Dickmann, 2024.

**How to Explain Coding to a Grown-Up**
by Ruth Spiro, 2023.

### Internet Sites

**Code.org**
*https://code.org/student/elementary*
Play games and learn how to use block code.

**Kiddle: Scratch Facts for Kids**
*https://kids.kiddle.co/
Scratch_(programming_language)*
Kiddle is an encyclopedia for kids with facts on many topics.

Every effort has been made to ensure that these websites are appropriate for children. However, because of the nature of the Internet, it is impossible to guarantee that these sites will remain active indefinitely or that their contents will not be altered.

# SHARE AND TAKE ACTION

**Complete more tutorials!**
Tutorials are a great way to learn coding. You can learn the skills you will need to make your dream coding project a reality.

**Explore other cool projects on Scratch.**
Then look inside to see the code. Can you understand the coder's logic?

**Draw your own characters.**
Upload them to use in your next coding project.

# GLOSSARY

**animation** A cartoon drawing or graphic that moves.

**bug** A mistake in a piece of code.

**debug** To find and remove mistakes or flaws from a computer program or code.

**platform** The hardware and software that allows a program to run.

**program** A set of instructions for a computer to follow so that it can do certain things.

**remix** To modify someone else's code to use in your own project.

**tutorial** A guided project with step-by-step instructions.

# INDEX



## About the Author

Jill Sherman writes books about pop stars, baby animals, and robots. She loves that writing allows her to research and learn about new topics. In addition to writing books, Jill sews her own clothes, creates crossword puzzles, and codes in JavaScript.